Roald Dahl's

Matilda

THE MUSICAL

MUSIC & LYRICS BY TIM MINCHIN

Roald Dahl's
Matilda
THE MUSICAL

BOOK
Dennis Kelly

MUSIC & LYRICS
Tim Minchin

ASSOCIATE CHOREOGRAPHER
Ellen Kane

ASSOCIATE DIRECTOR
Luke Sheppard

ASSOCIATE DIRECTOR
Lotte Wakeham

COMMISSIONING DRAMATURG
Jeanie O'Hare

CASTING
David Grindrod CDG
Hannah Miller CDG

CHILDREN'S CASTING
Jessica Ronane CDG

MUSICAL DIRECTOR
Alan Berry

EXECUTIVE PRODUCER
André Ptaszynski

EXECUTIVE PRODUCER
Denise Wood

ORCHESTRATION & ADDITIONAL MUSIC
Christopher Nightingale

SOUND DESIGN
Simon Baker

LIGHTING DESIGN
Hugh Vanstone

ILLUSION
Paul Kieve

SET & COSTUME DESIGN
Rob Howell

CHOREOGRAPHY
Peter Darling

DIRECTOR
Matthew Warchus

Roald Dahl's
Matilda
THE MUSICAL

MUSIC & LYRICS BY TIM MINCHIN

ISBN 978-1-78305-036-9

Visit Hal Leonard Online at
www.halleonard.com

World headquarters, contact:
Hal Leonard
7777 West Bluemound Road
Milwaukee, WI 53213
Email: info@halleonard.com

In Europe, contact:
Hal Leonard Europe Limited
1 Red Place
London, W1K 6PL
Email: info@halleonardeurope.com

In Australia, contact:
Hal Leonard Australia Pty. Ltd.
4 Lentara Court
Cheltenham, Victoria, 3192 Australia
Email: info@halleonard.com.au

Order No. AM1006401

Edited by Jenni Norey.
Music arranged by Vasco Hexel.
Music processed by Paul Ewers Music Design.
Photographs of the original London cast at the Cambridge Theatre
by Manuel Harlan. © Royal Shakespeare Company.
Cover image artwork and design by aka.
Printed in the UK.

First performance at The Courtyard Theatre,
Stratford-upon-Avon, 9 November 2010

First performance at The Cambridge Theatre,
London, 25 October 2011

First performance at The Shubert Theatre,
New York, 4 March 2013

First performance at Sydney Lyric Theatre,
Australia, 28 July 2015

With thanks to Tim Minchin, Chris Nightingale,
Caroline Chignell and Kevin Wright.

Naughty

Words & Music by Tim Minchin

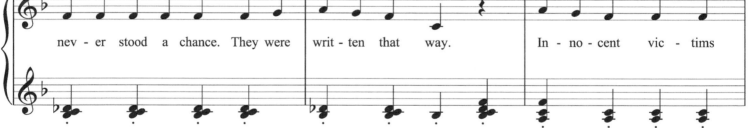

Ro-me-o and Ju-li-et: 'twas writ-ten in the stars be-fore they e-ven met that

love and fate and a touch of stu-pi-di-ty would rob them of their

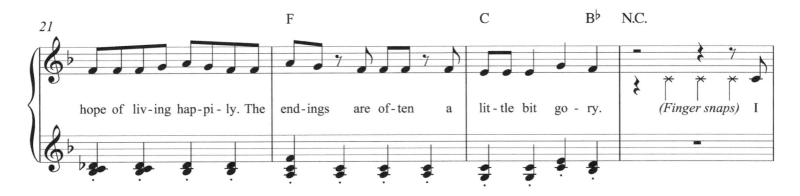

hope of liv-ing hap-pi-ly. The end-ings are of-ten a lit-tle bit go-ry. *(Finger snaps)* I

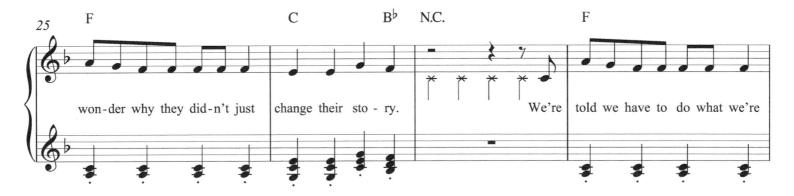

won-der why they did-n't just change their sto-ry. We're told we have to do what we're

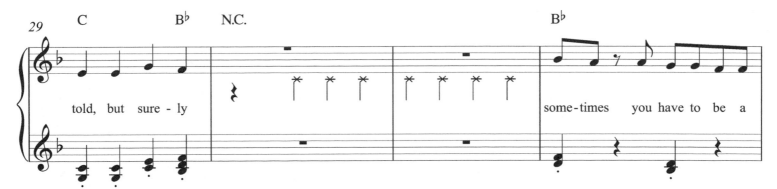

told, but sure-ly some-times you have to be a

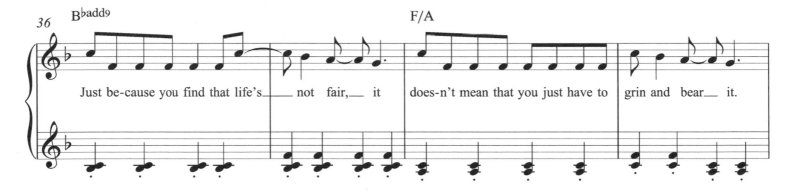

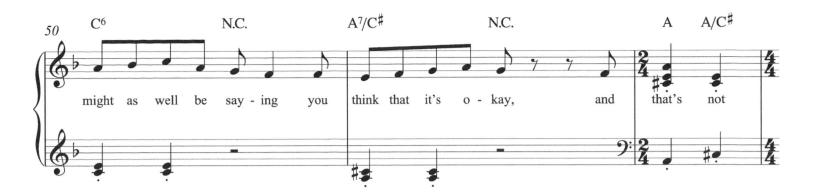

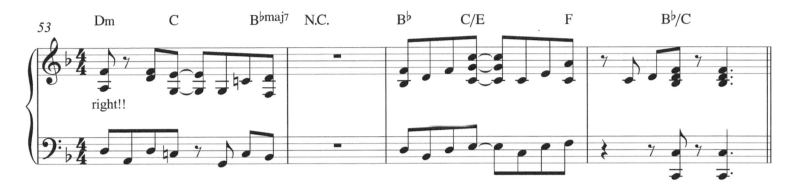

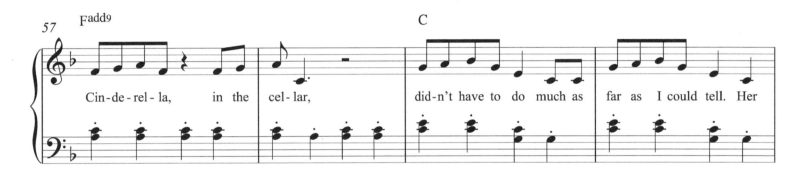

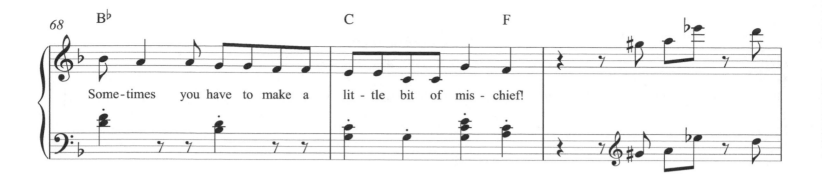

Some-times you have to make a lit-tle bit of mis-chief!

Just be-cause you find that life's___ not fair,___ it does-n't mean that you just have to

grin and bear___ it. If you al-ways take it on the chin and wear it, noth-ing will change.

E-ven if you're lit-tle you can do a lot,___ you must-n't let a lit-tle thing like

lit-tle stop_ you. If you sit a-round and let them get on top,_ you might as well be say-ing you

think that it's o-kay, and that's not right! And if it's not

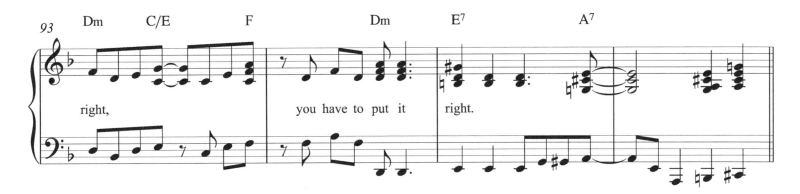

right, you have to put it right.

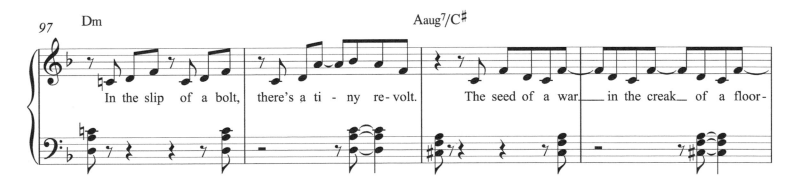

In the slip of a bolt, there's a ti-ny re-volt. The seed of a war_ in the creak_ of a floor-

-board. A storm can be-gin with the flap of a wing. The ti-ni-est mite_ packs the might-i-est

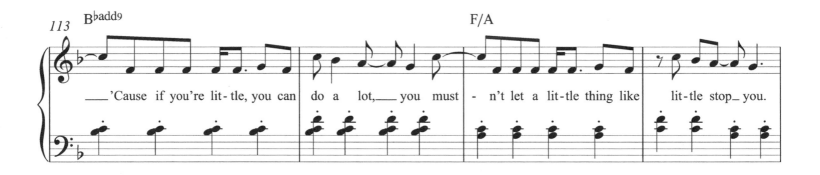

If you al-ways take it on the chin and wear it, you might as well be say-ing you

think that it's o-kay. And that's not right. And if it's not

right, you have to put it right. But

no-bod-y else___ is gon-na put it right for me. No-bod-y but me is gon-na

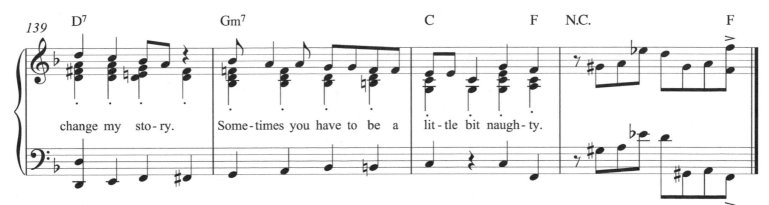

change my sto-ry. Some-times you have to be a lit-tle bit naugh-ty.

School Song

Words & Music by Tim Minchin

♩ = c. 105

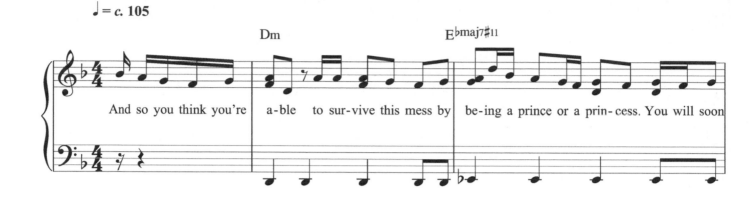

And so you think you're a-ble to sur-vive this mess by be-ing a prince or a prin-cess. You will soon

see there's no es-cap-ing tra-ge - dy. And e - ven if you put in heaps of

ef- fort, you're just wast-ing en-er - gy, 'cause your life as you know it is an-cient his-to - ry.

I have suf-fered in this jail.— Have been trapped in-side this cage for a-ges, this liv-ing

'ell. But if I try I can re-mem-ber, back be-fore my life had end-ed, be-fore my hap-py days were

o-ver, be-fore I first heard the peal-ing of the bell. Like you I was

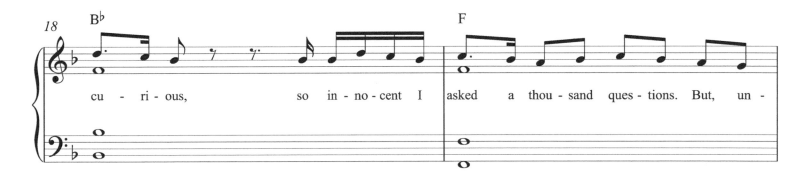

cu-ri-ous, so in-no-cent I asked a thou-sand ques-tions. But, un-

-less you want to suf-fer, lis-ten up and I will teach you a thing or two.

You lis-ten here, my dear, you'll be pu-nished so se-vere-ly if you step out of line. And if you cry it will be

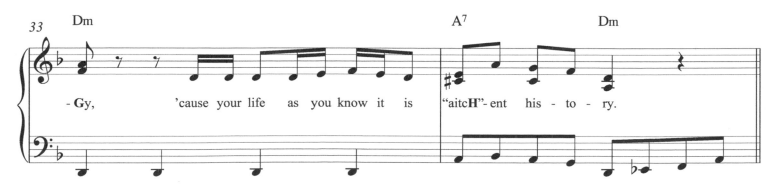

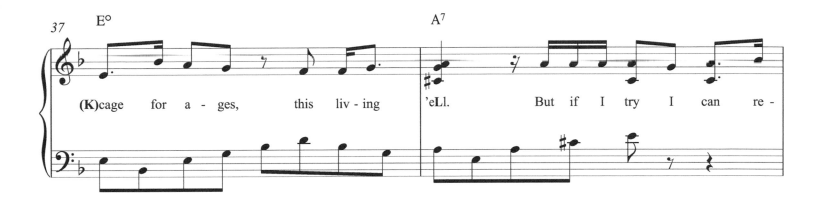

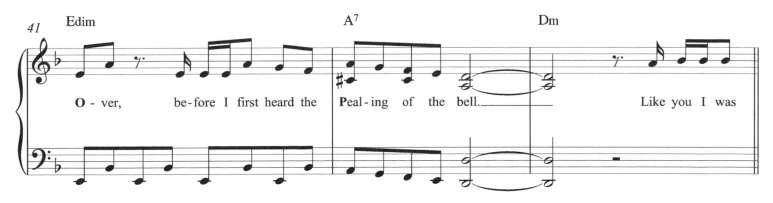

(Q)cu - ri - ous,   so in - no - cent I   (R)asked a thou - sand ques - tions. But, un -

-leSs you want to suf - fer, lis - ten up and I will Teach you   a thing or two.

YoU lis-ten here,   my dear, you'll be pu - nished so se - Vere-ly if you step out of line. And if you cry it will be

(W)dou - ble. You should stay out of trou-ble and re-mem-ber to be eX-treme-ly care - ful.   WhY?

26

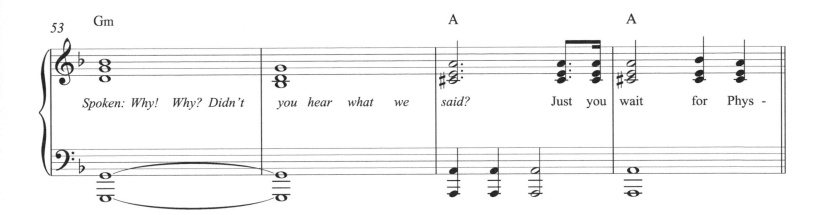

Spoken: Why! Why? Didn't you hear what we said? Just you wait for Phys -

- Ed!_____ Just you wait for Phys -

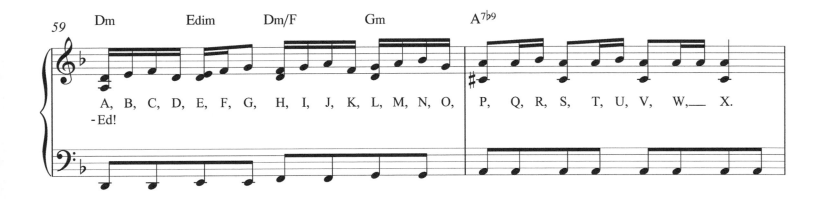

A, B, C, D, E, F, G, H, I, J, K, L, M, N, O, P, Q, R, S, T, U, V, W,__ X.
-Ed!

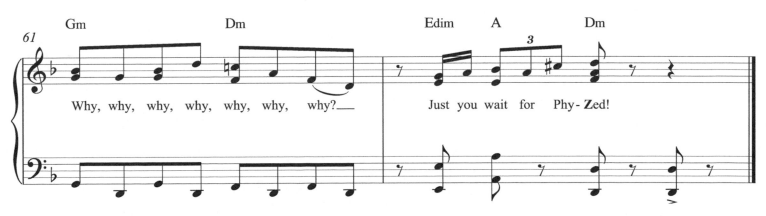

Why, why, why, why, why, why, why?__ Just you wait for Phy- **Zed!**

The Hammer

Words & Music by Tim Minchin

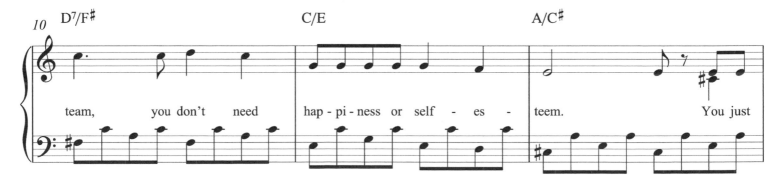

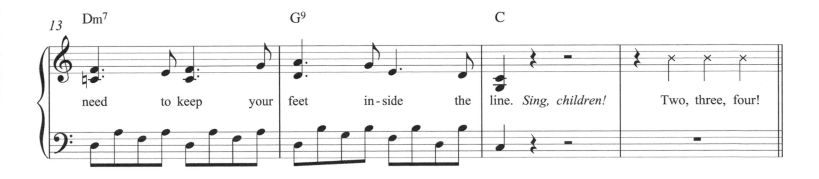

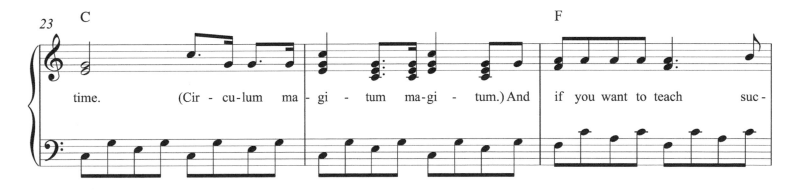

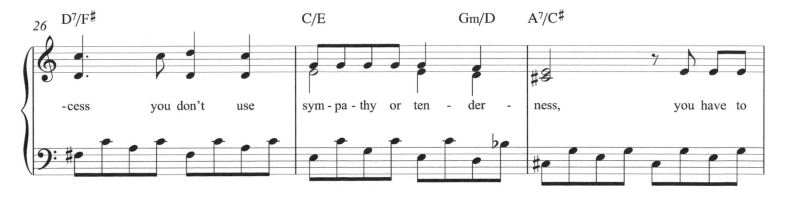

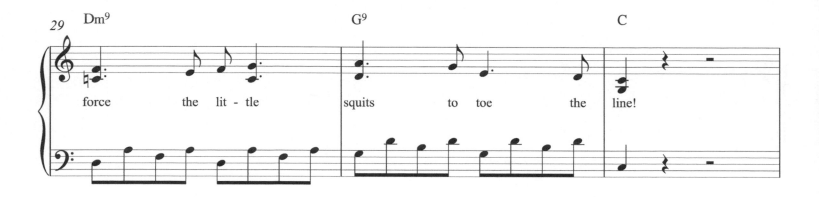

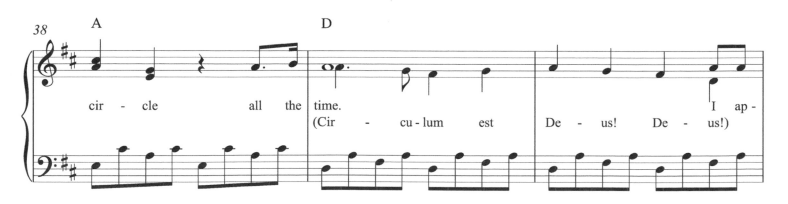

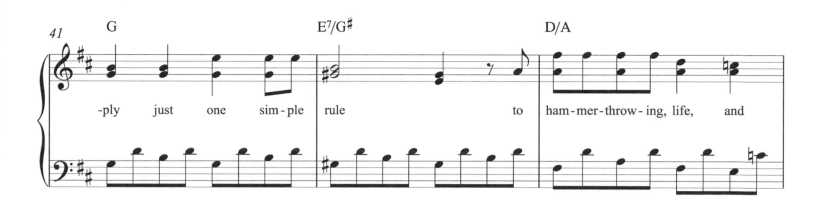

-ply just one sim-ple rule to ham-mer-throw-ing, life, and

school. Life's a ball, so learn to throw it,

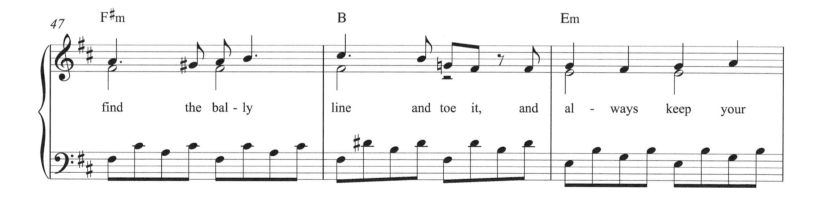

find the bal-ly line and toe it, and al - ways keep your

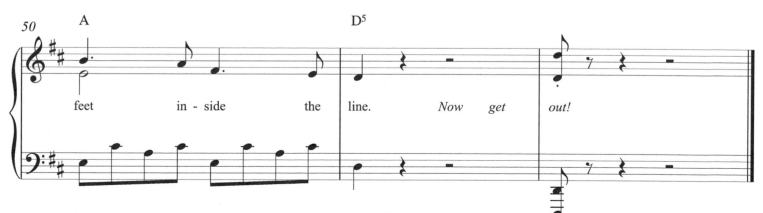

feet in - side the line. *Now get out!*

Bruce

Words & Music by Tim Minchin

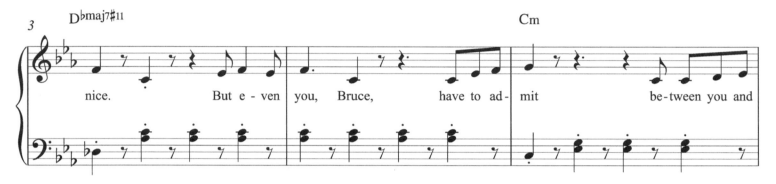

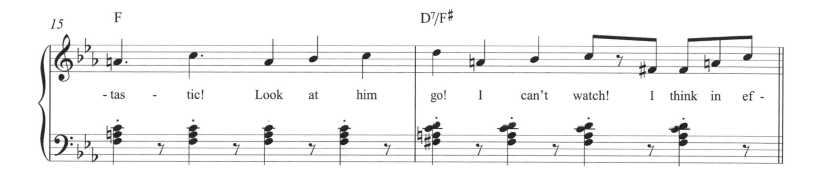

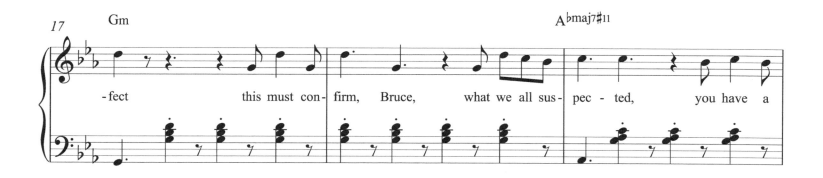

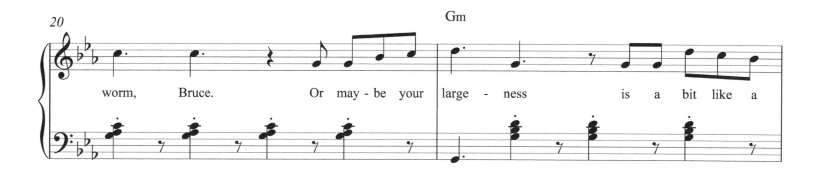

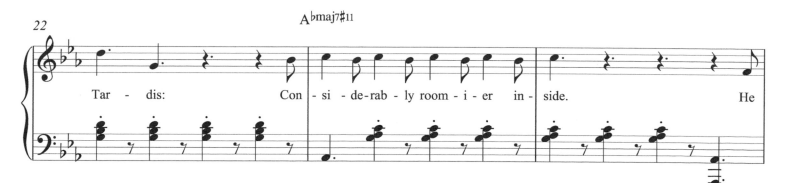

33

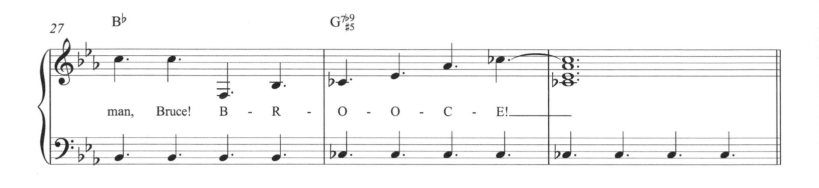

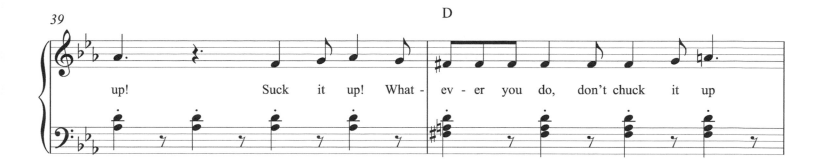

up!   Suck   it   up!   What - ev - er   you   do,   don't   chuck   it   up

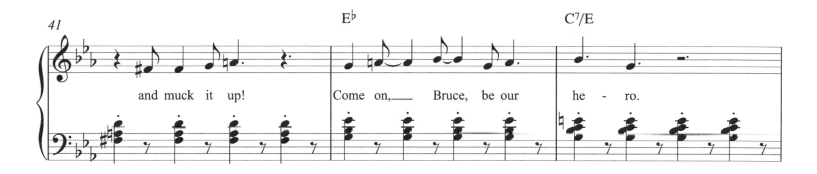

and   muck   it   up!   Come   on,___   Bruce,   be   our   he - ro.

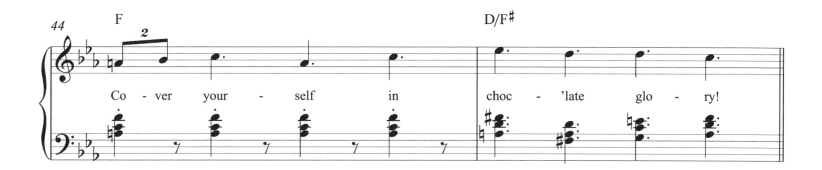

Co - ver   your - self   in   choc - 'late   glo - ry!

Bruce!   You'll   nev - er   a-gain   be   sub - ject   to   a-buse   for   your   im-

-mense   ca - boose!   She'll   call   a   truce,   Bruce.   With   ev - 'ry   swal - low   you   are

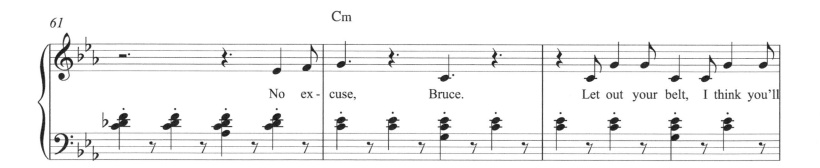

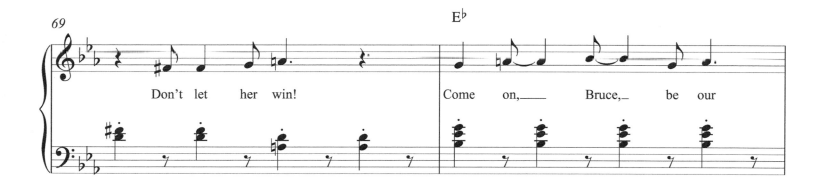

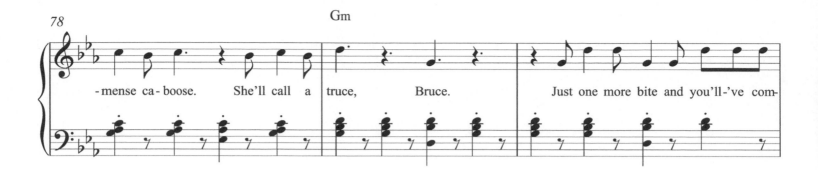

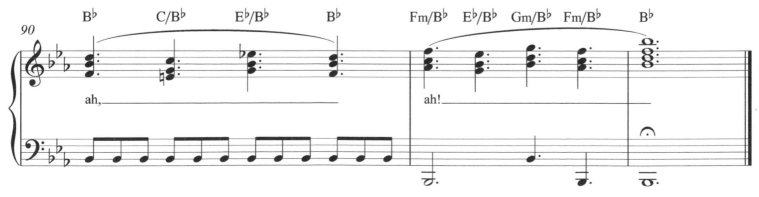

Telly

Words & Music by Tim Minchin

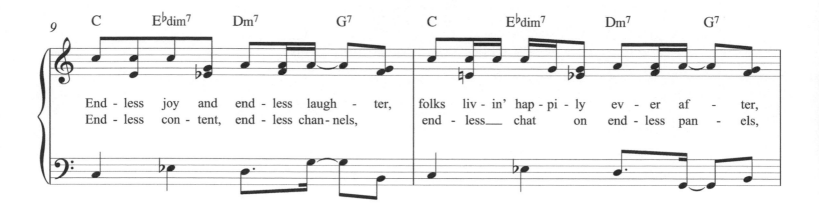

End - less joy and end - less laugh - ter, folks liv - in' hap - pi - ly ev - er af - ter,
End - less con - tent, end - less chan - nels, end - less__ chat on end - less pan - els,

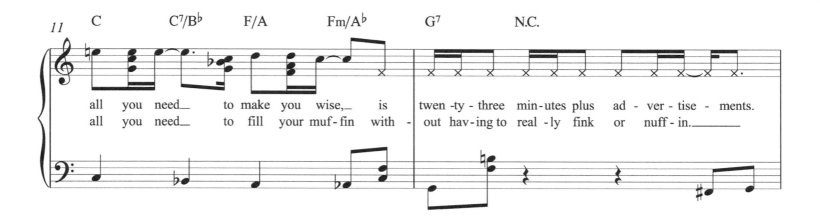

all you need__ to make you wise,__ is twen - ty - three min - utes plus ad - ver - tise - ments.
all you need__ to fill your muf - fin with - out hav - ing to real - ly fink or nuff - in._____

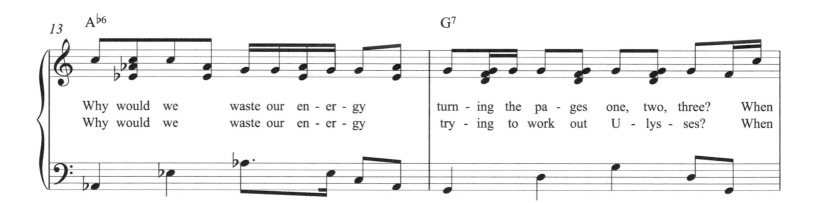

Why would we waste our en - er - gy turn - ing the pa - ges one, two, three? When
Why would we waste our en - er - gy try - ing to work out U - lys - ses? When

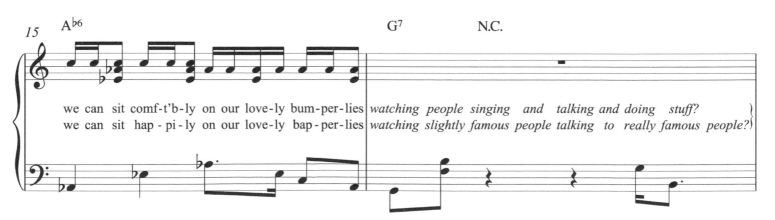

we can sit comf - t'b - ly on our love - ly bum - per - lies *watching people singing and talking and doing stuff?*
we can sit hap - pi - ly on our love - ly bap - per - lies *watching slightly famous people talking to really famous people?*

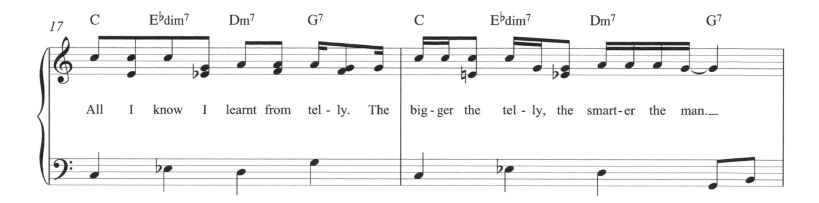

All I know I learnt from tel - ly. The big - ger the tel - ly, the smart - er the man.___

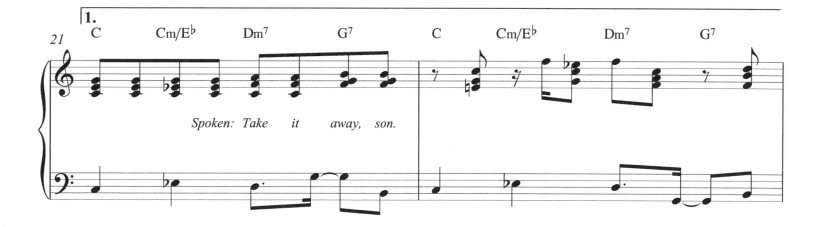

You can tell from my big tel - ly just what a clev - er fel - la I am.

1.

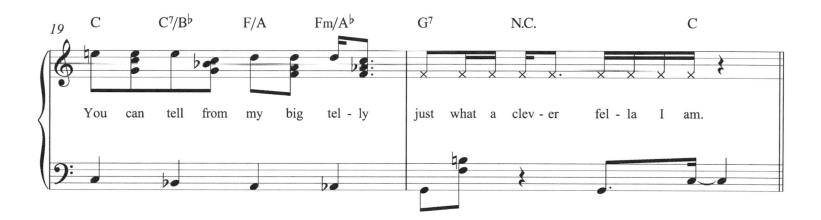

Spoken: Take it away, son.

2.

You can't learn from a stupid book.

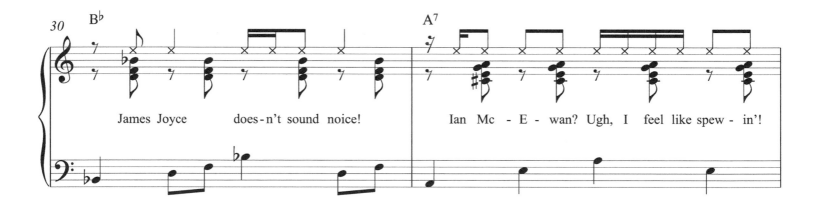

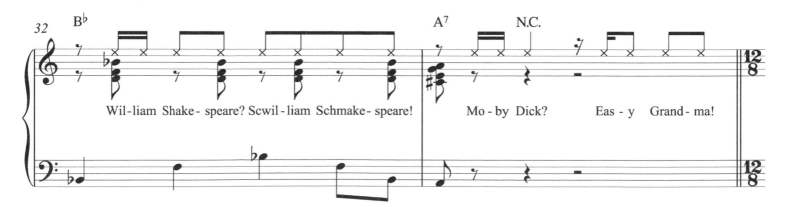

Spoken: All together now!

All I know___ I

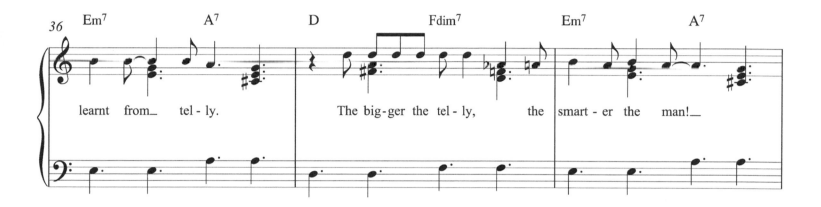

learnt from___ tel - ly.   The big - ger the tel - ly,   the smart - er the man!___

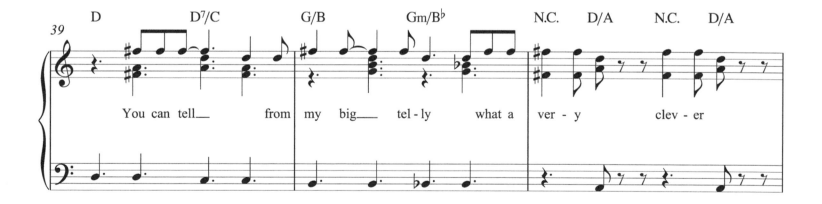

You can tell___   from my big___ tel - ly what a ver - y   clev - er

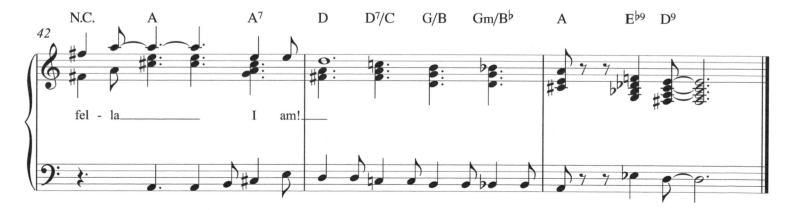

fel - la_____   I am!___

When I Grow Up

Words & Music by Tim Minchin

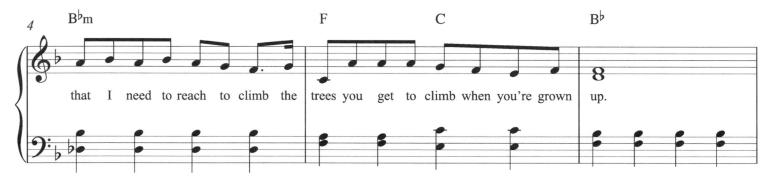

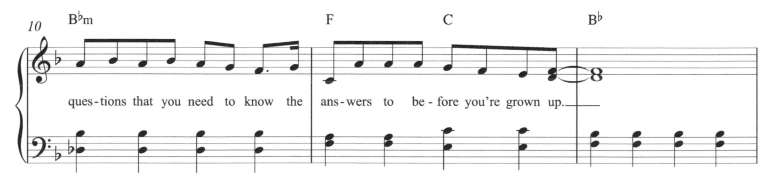

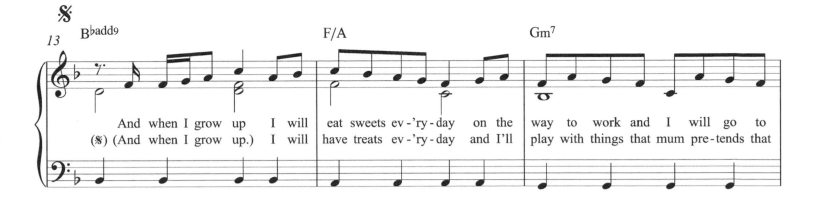

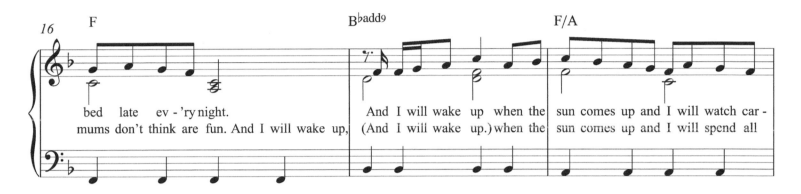

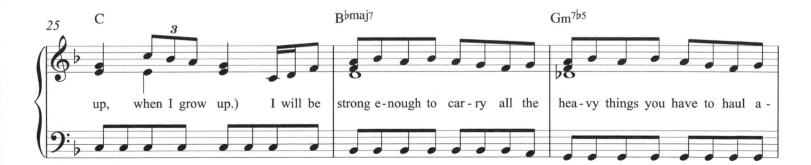

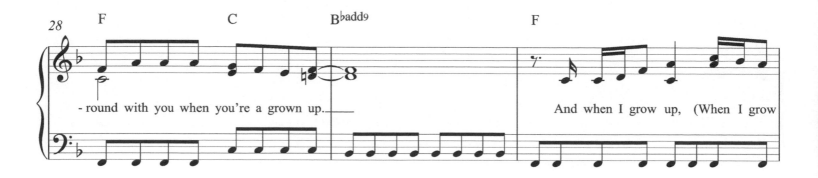

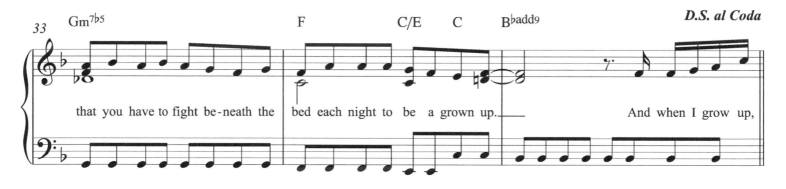

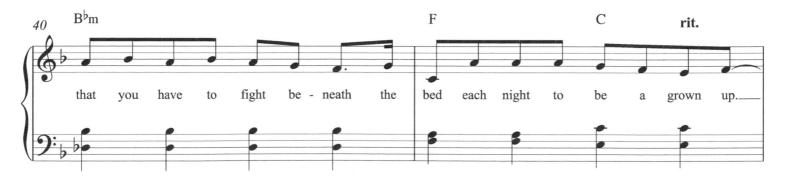

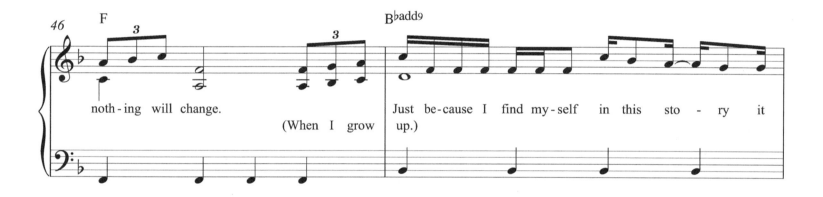

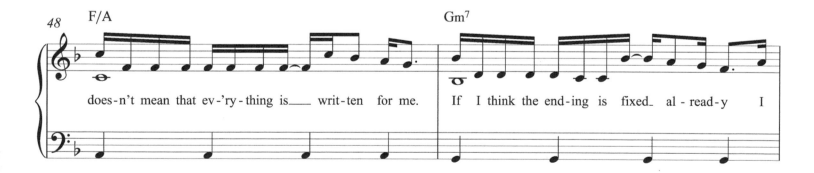

The Smell Of Rebellion

Words & Music by Tim Minchin

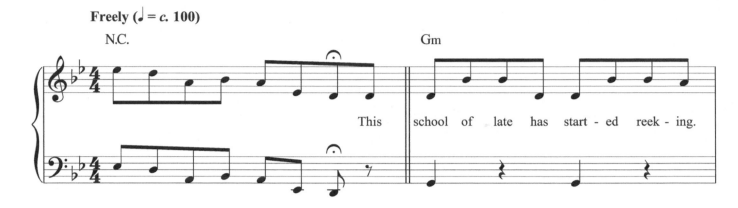

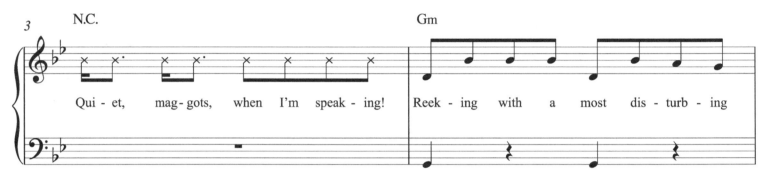

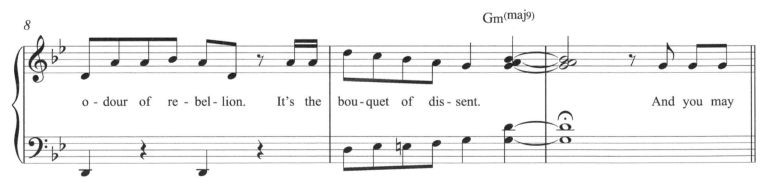

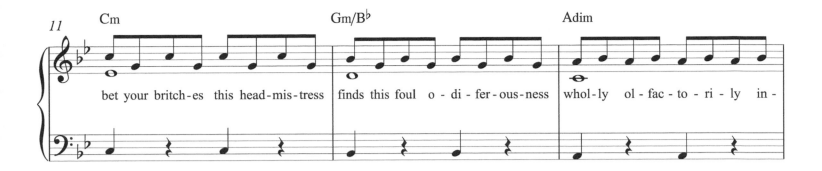

bet your britch-es this head-mis-tress | finds this foul o - di - fer-ous-ness | whol - ly ol -fac -to - ri - ly in -

-sult - ing. And | so, to stop the stench's spread, I | find a ses -sion of Phys - Ed

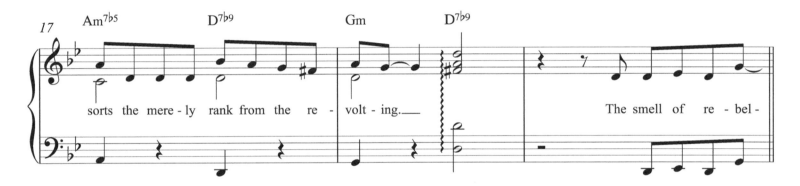

sorts the mere -ly rank from the re - | volt - ing.___ | The smell of re -bel-

Slight swing (♩ = c. 120)

- lion comes out in the sweat___ | and Phys - Ed will get you sweat-ing.

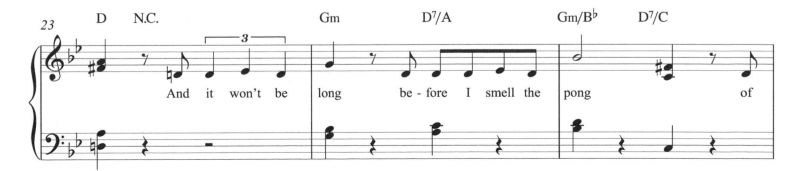

And it won't be | long be -fore I smell the | pong of

aid-ing and a-bet-ting._ A bit of Phys- Ed will tell us who has a

head full of re-bel-li-lous thoughts. Hold! Hold! Just like a

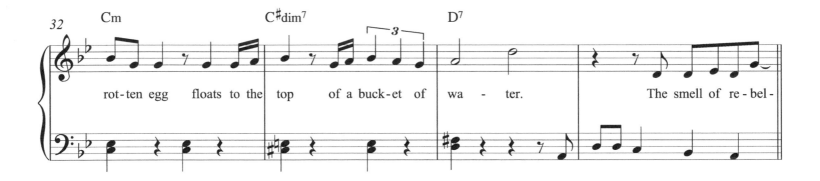

rot-ten egg floats to the top of a buck-et of wa - ter. The smell of re-bel-

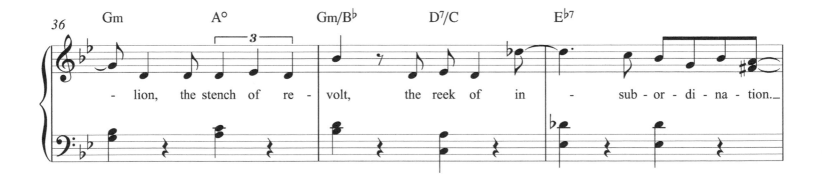

- lion, the stench of re - volt, the reek of in - sub-or-di-na-tion._

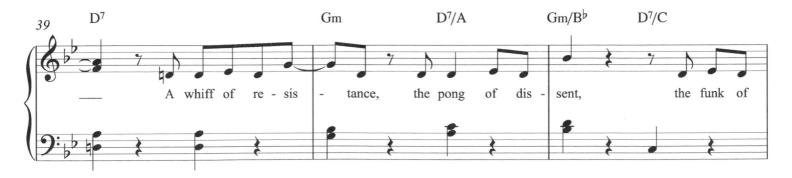

_ A whiff of re-sis - tance, the pong of dis - sent, the funk of

mu - ti - ny in ac - tion.   Be - fore a   weed___ be-comes too big and

greed - y,   you real - ly need to   nip it in the bud. Po - si - tion   two!   Be - fore the

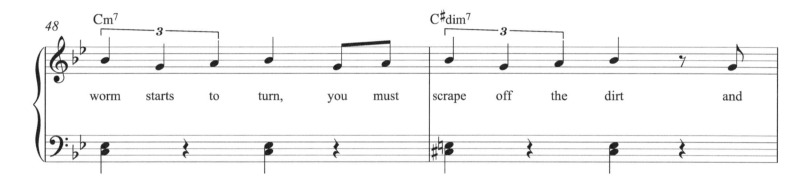

worm starts to turn,   you must   scrape off the dirt   and

rip it from the mud.   The whiff of in - sur -

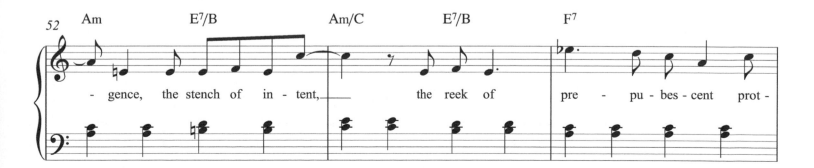

- gence, the stench of in - tent,___   the reek of   pre - pu - bes - cent prot -

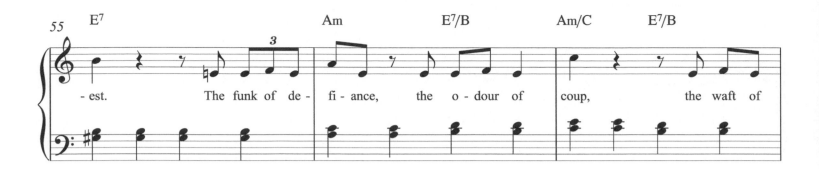

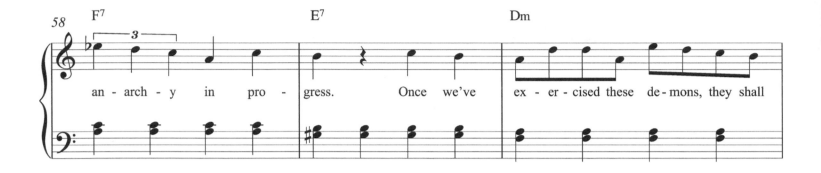

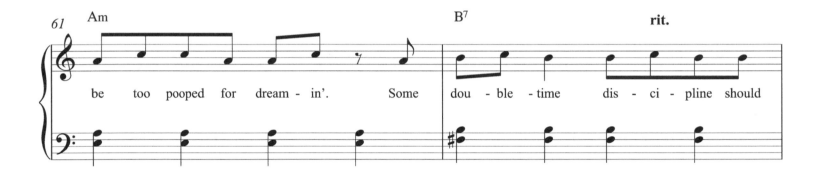

Straight, a tempo (♪ = ♩)

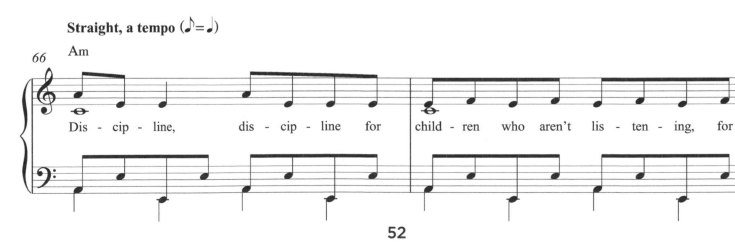

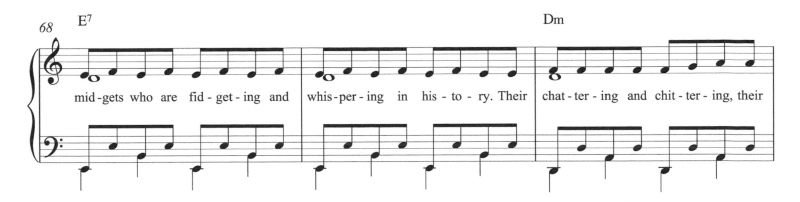

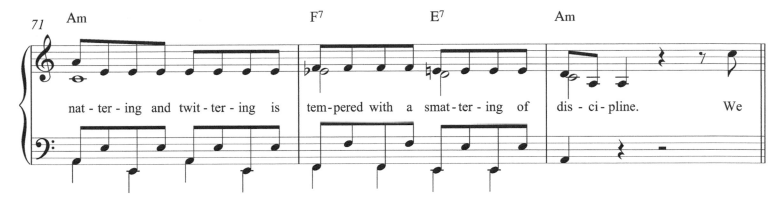

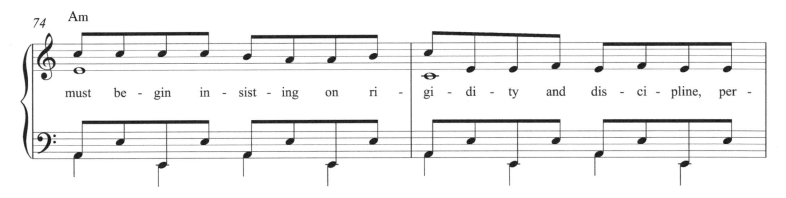

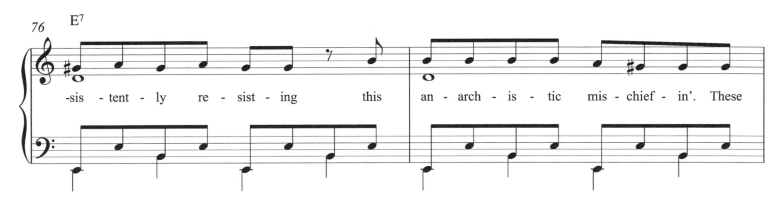

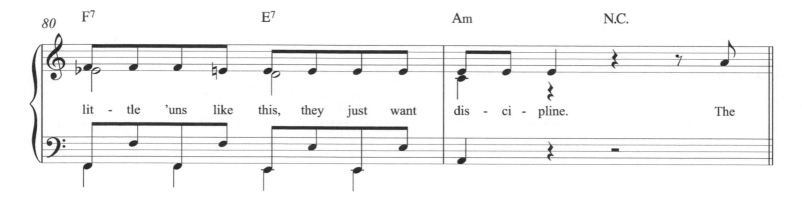

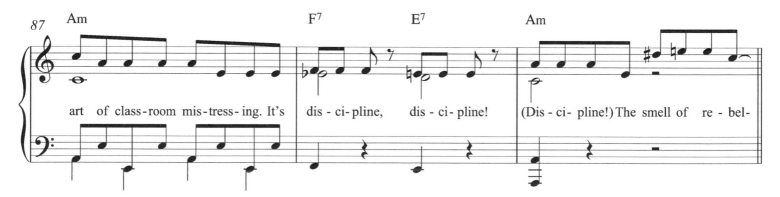

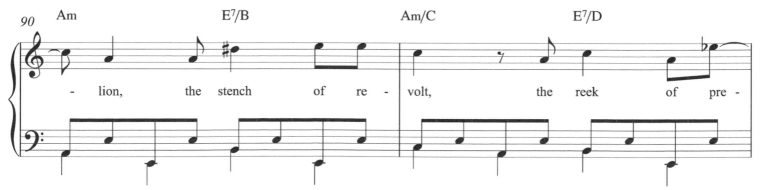

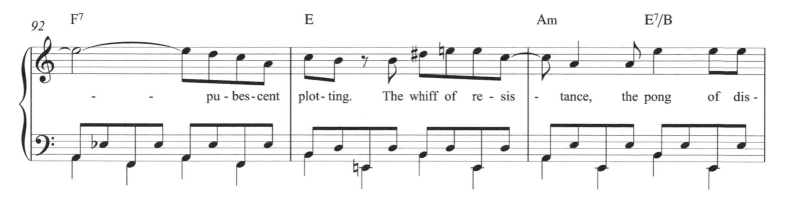

92

F⁷ — — pu - bes - cent plot - ting. E The whiff of re - sis - tance, Am the pong E⁷/B of dis -

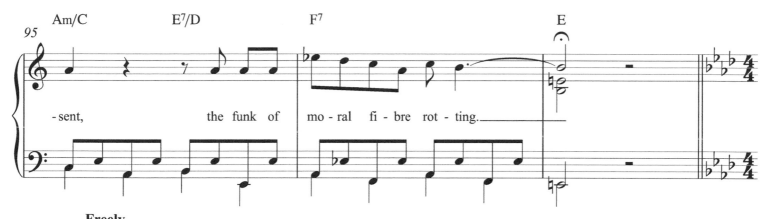

95

Am/C - sent, E⁷/D the funk of F⁷ mo - ral fi - bre rot - ting. E

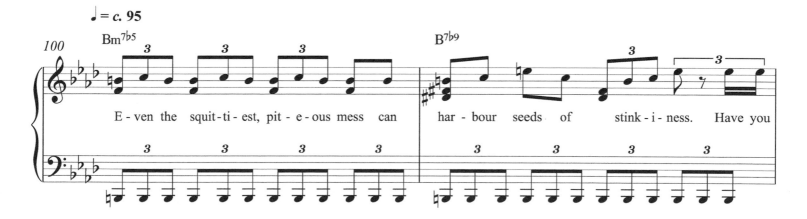

Freely

98

Dm(maj7) And there, just like I said, the Am(maj7)/C stink - y mag - got rears his head.

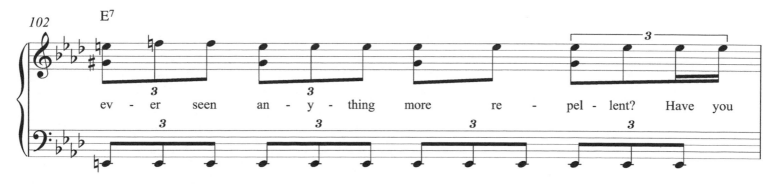

♩ = c. 95

100

Bm⁷♭⁵ E - ven the squit - ti - est, pit - e - ous mess can B⁷♭⁹ har - bour seeds of stink - i - ness. Have you

102

E⁷ ev - er seen an - y - thing more re - pel - lent? Have you

ev - er smelled an - y - thing worse than that smell of re -

Swing (♩ = *c.* 100)

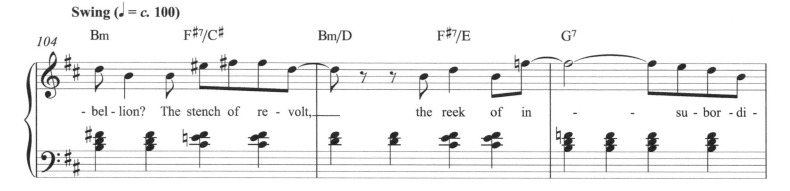

- bel - lion? The stench of re - volt,___ the reek of in - - su - bor - di -

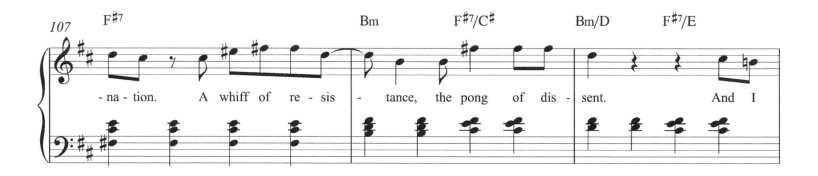

- na - tion. A whiff of re - sis - tance, the pong of dis - sent. And I

will not stop till you are squashed. Till this re - bel - li - on is quashed. Till glo - rious, sweat - y dis - ci - pline has

washed this sick - en - ing scent a - way!

Quiet

Words & Music by Tim Minchin

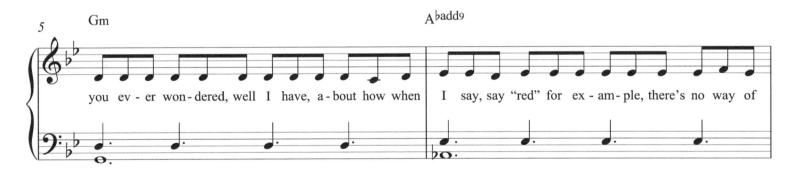

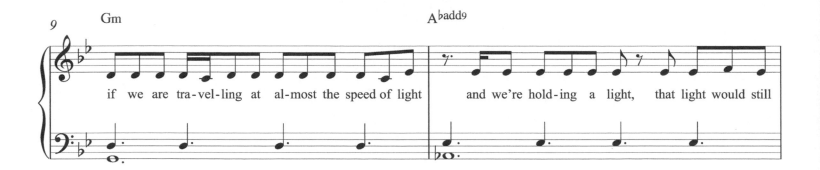

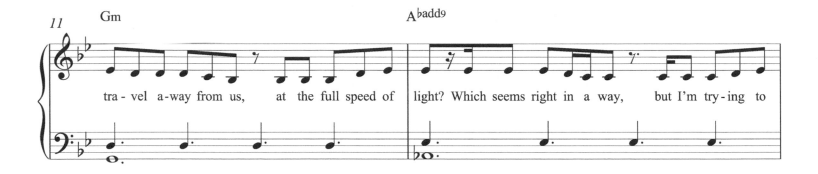

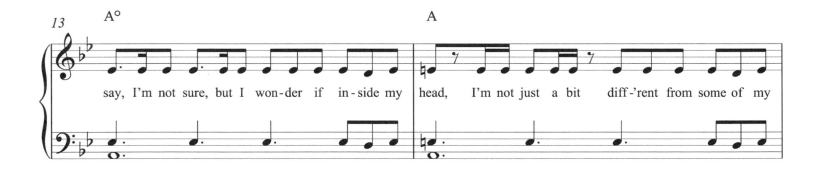

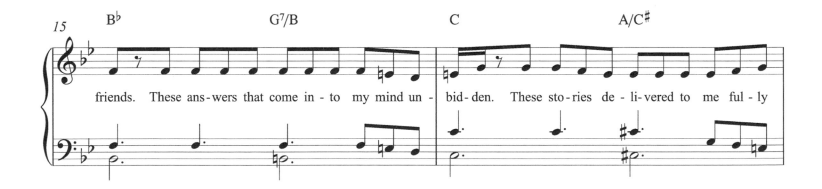

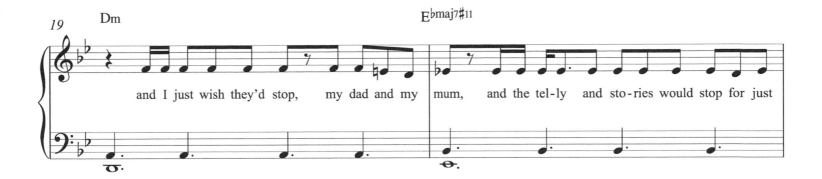

and I just wish they'd stop, my dad and my mum, and the tel-ly and sto-ries would stop for just

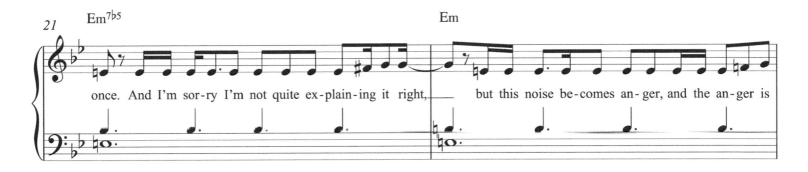

once. And I'm sor-ry I'm not quite ex-plain-ing it right, but this noise be-comes an-ger, and the an-ger is

light, and this burn-ing in-side me would us-ual-ly fade, but it is-n't to-day, and the heat and the

shout-ing, and my heart is pound-ing, and my eyes are burn-ing, and sud-den-ly ev-'ry-thing, ev-'ry-thing

is... Qui-et.___ Like si-lence, but not real-ly

si - lent.＿ Just that still sort of qui - et like the sound of a page＿

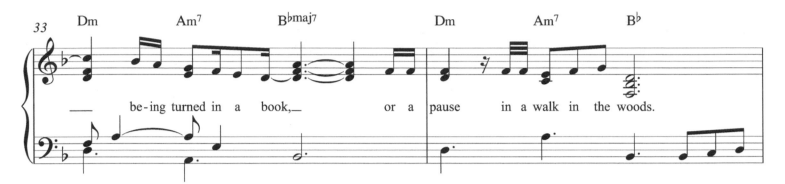

＿ be-ing turned in a book,＿ or a pause in a walk in the woods.

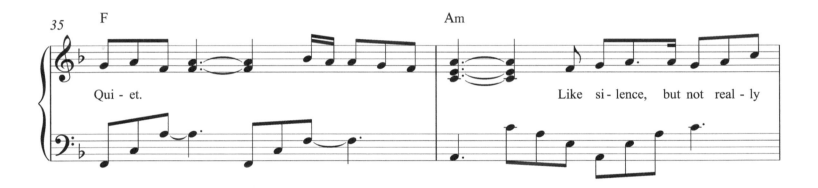

Qui - et. Like si - lence, but not real - ly

si - lent. Just that nice kind of qui - et like the sound when you

lie up-side down in your bed. Just the sound of your heart in your head. And though the

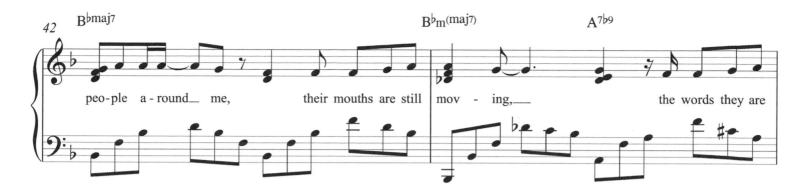

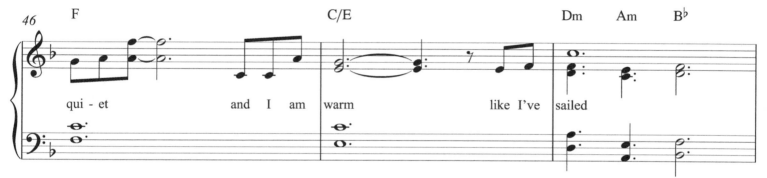

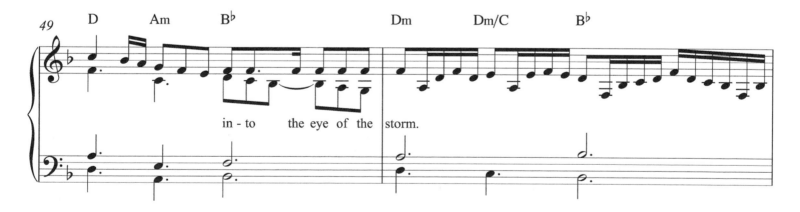

My House

Words & Music by Tim Minchin

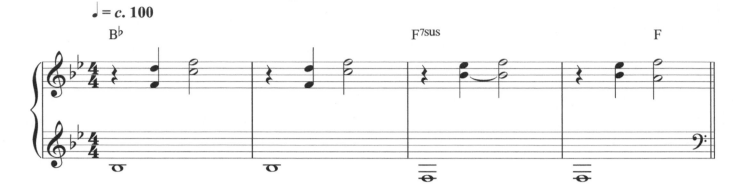

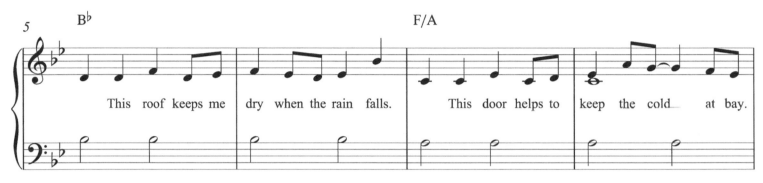

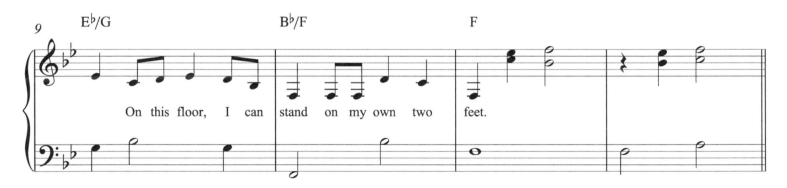

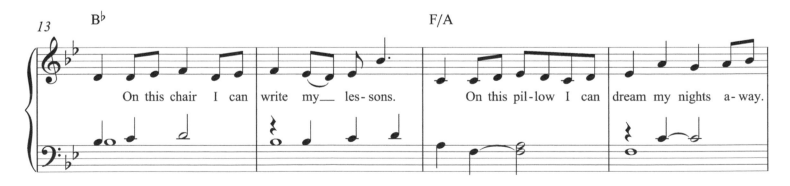

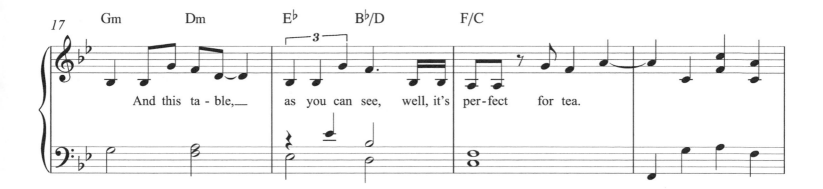

And this ta - ble,___ as you can see, well, it's per - fect for tea.

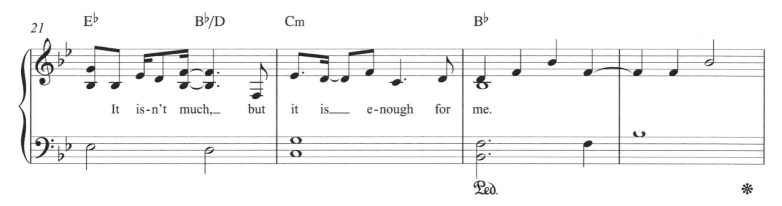

It is-n't much,___ but it is___ e-nough for me.

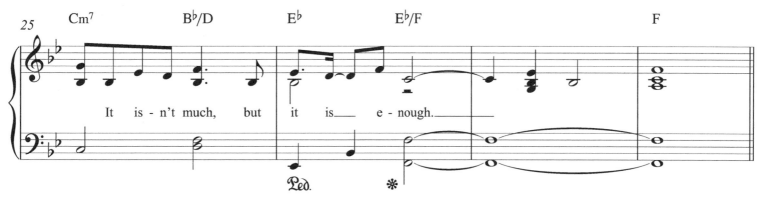

It is - n't much, but it is___ e - nough.___

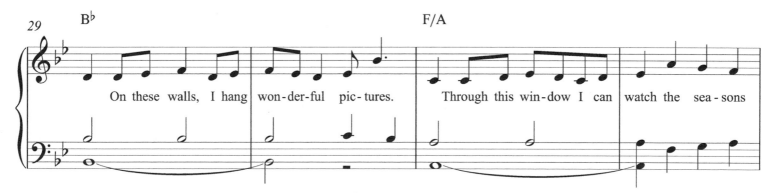

On these walls, I hang won-der-ful pic-tures. Through this win-dow I can watch the sea-sons

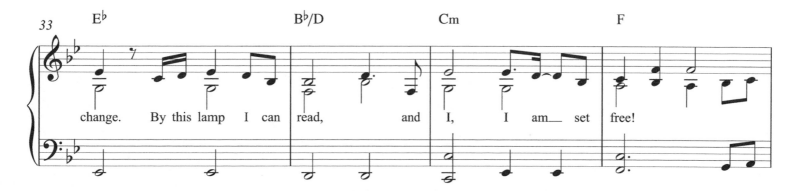

change. By this lamp I can read, and I, I am___ set free!

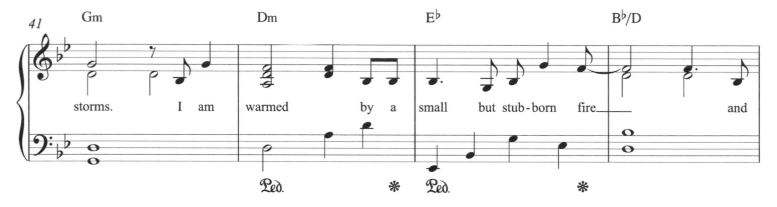

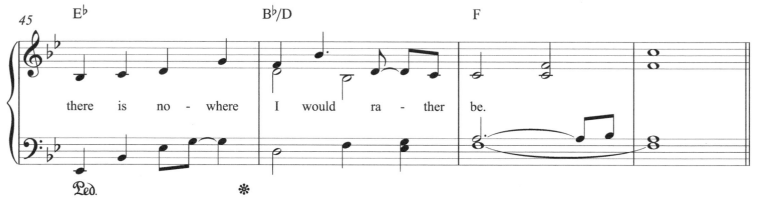

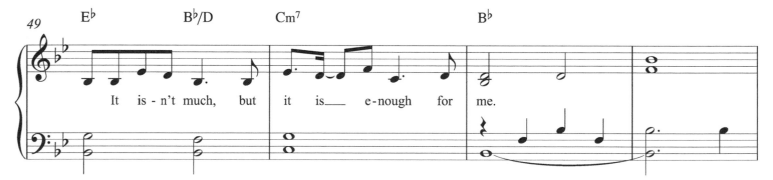

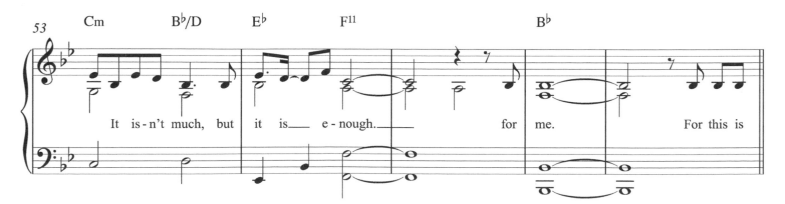

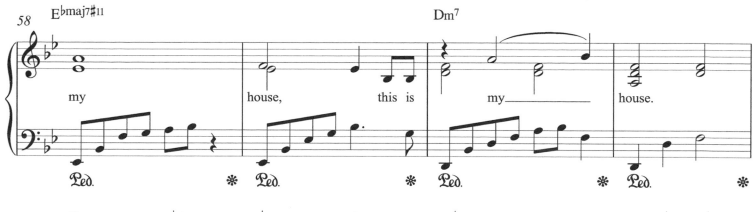

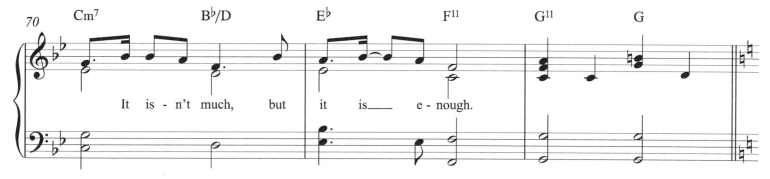

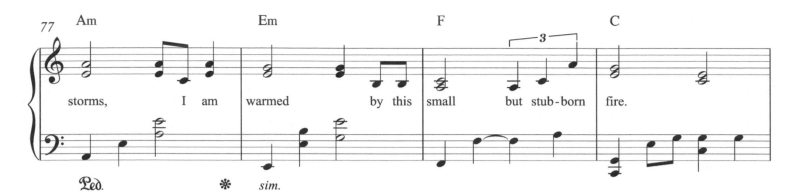

storms, I am warmed by this small but stub-born fire.

E - ven when out - side it's freez- ing, I don't pay much heed. I know that

ev - 'ry - thing I need is in here.

It is - n't much, but it is e - nough for me.

poco rit.

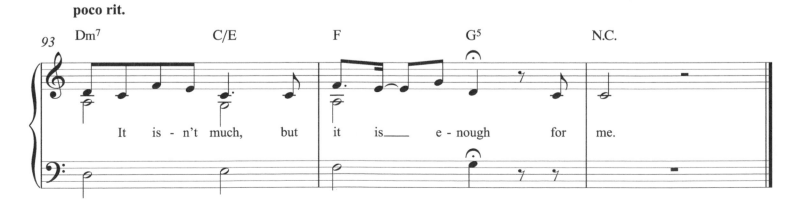

It is - n't much, but it is e - nough for me.

Revolting Children

Words & Music by Tim Minchin

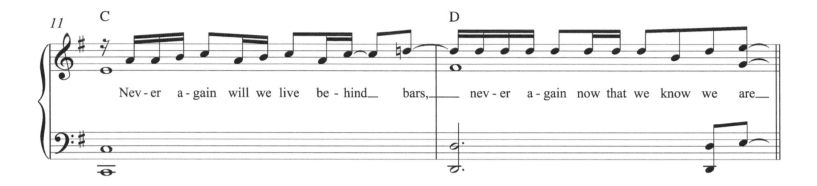

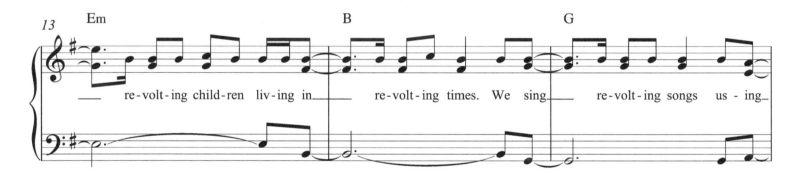

re-volt-ing child-ren liv-ing in _____ re-volt-ing times. We sing _____ re-volt-ing songs us-ing

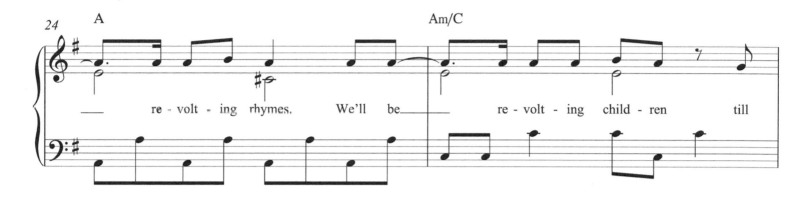

_____ re - volt - ing rhymes. We'll be _____ re - volt - ing chil - dren till

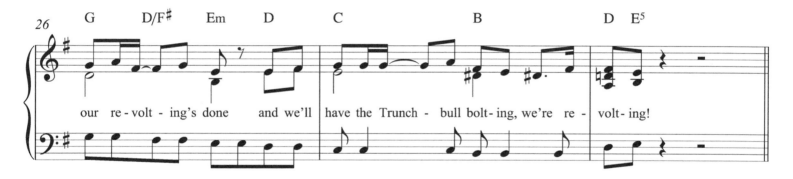

our re - volt - ing's done and we'll have the Trunch - bull bolt - ing, we're re - volt - ing!

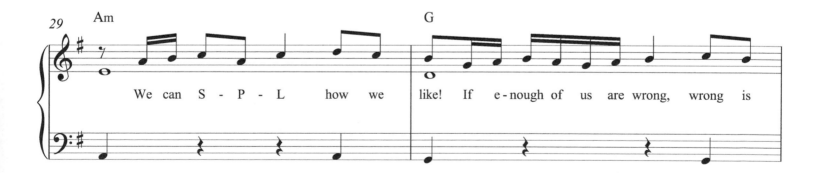

We can S - P - L how we like! If e - nough of us are wrong, wrong is

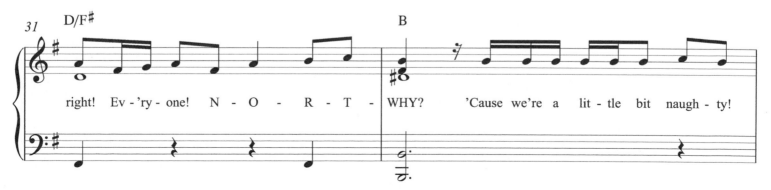

right! Ev - 'ry - one! N - O - R - T - WHY? 'Cause we're a lit - tle bit naugh - ty!

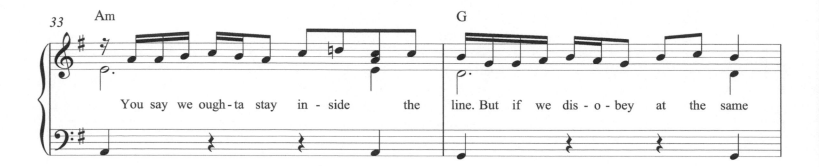

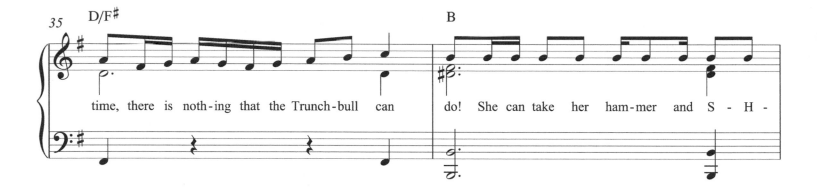

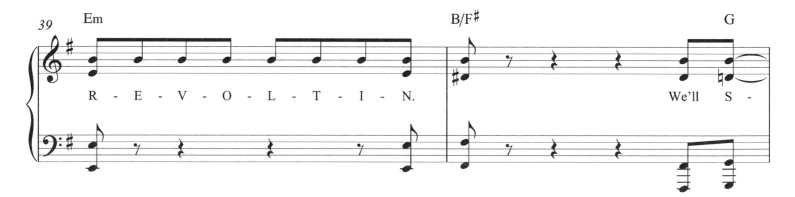

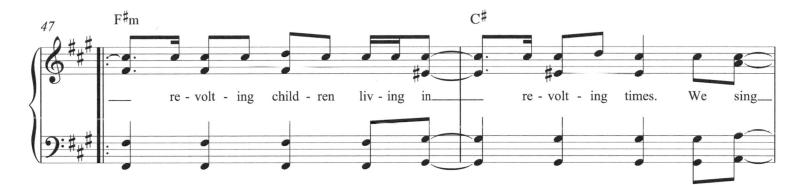

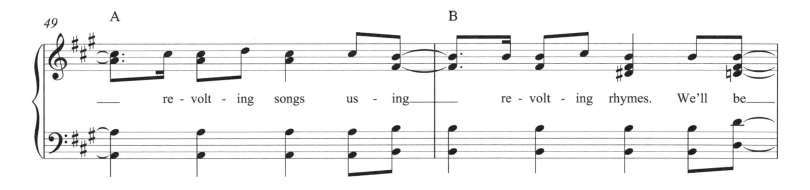

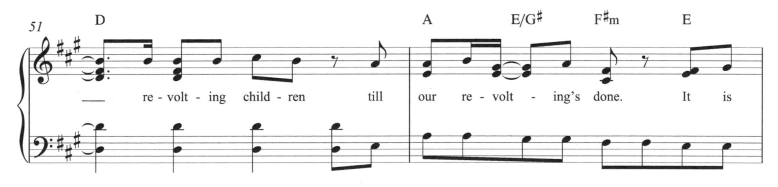

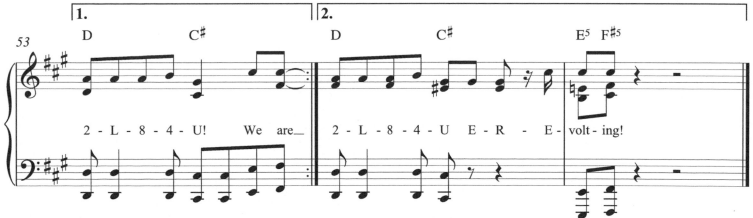

Also available

THE MUSICAL

Original Cast Recording

The original cast recording of the Royal Shakespeare Company's production of MATILDA THE MUSICAL.

CD available from:

www.matildathemusical.com

RSCE 002